CONTENTS

SAFE HOUSES

During the Middle Ages — which lasted from about the 700s to 1500 AD — there were thousands of castles in western Europe. They were owned by the rich and powerful because only they could afford such splendid homes. Although many of these castles were never even threatened with attack, all were designed to repel the weapons of their day. They were like homely forts, built to protect their owner and his land, his family, his servants, his crafts people and his private army of knights.

CASTLE SITES

Where possible, castles were built on or near natural defences such as cliffs and coastlines. Many were founded near the port, town or crossroads they were designed to protect or control. Some were built near rivers and streams. A ditch could then be dug around the finished castle and the water diverted into it. These water-filled ditches, called moats, made castles much harder to attack.

▲ *This painting of Lusignan Castle in France is taken from the Duke of Berry's* The Book of Hours *which was made in 1400.*

▶ *Many wooden castles had gatehouses and moveable bridges to guard the main entrance and the approach to the tower.*

CRAFT TOPICS

CASTLES

FACTS ● THINGS TO MAKE ● ACTIVITIES

RACHEL WRIGHT

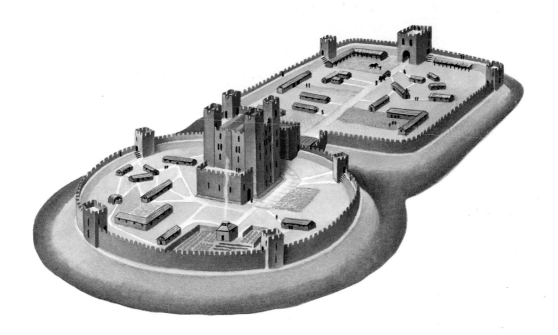

W

FRANKLIN WATTS

LONDON●SYDNEY

© 1992 Franklin Watts
This edition 2002

Franklin Watts
96 Leonard Street
London
EC2A 4XD

Franklin Watts Australia
56 O'Riordan Street
Alexandria, Sydney
NSW 2015

ISBN 0 7496 4551 2 (pbk)

Dewey Decimal Classification 728.8

Editor: Hazel Poole
Designer: Sally Boothroyd
Photographer: Chris Fairclough

A CIP catalogue record for this book is
available from the British Library

Printed in Dubai

Castles were often closely linked with a neighbouring town or village. As well as being a rich man's home, they acted as a tax office, administration centre, courthouse and prison for local villagers.

WOODEN CASTLES

In some parts of Europe, the first castles were made of earth and wood. Often a steep-sided flat topped mound of earth was dug, surrounded by a ditch. A wooden tower was then built on top of the mound and encircled by a timber fence. This tower was the strong point of the castle and the place where valuables were kept.

The castle's owner and his family slept in apartments beside the Great Hall, in the courtyard below. The rest of the domestic buildings, including the kitchen, the chapel and the stables, also stood in the courtyard. These buildings were usually timber-framed and plastered over with earth and animal dung. The more important ones were roofed with tiles or shingles. The others were thatched with reeds or straw.

◀ *The castle at Peñafiel in Spain was built on top of a rocky ridge for protection. "Peña fiel" means "faithful rock."*

Wooden castles were cheaper, quicker and required less skill to build than stone ones, but they had two major disadvantages. They rotted and burned easily. For those who wanted a more permanent home, the only solution was to build in stone.

5

PULP AND PAPER CASTLES

You will need: newspaper
● wallpaper paste ● glue brush
● large bowl of warm water
● corrugated card ● scissors ● ruler
● pencil ● glue ● paint ● some
wood or hardboard to use as a
baseboard ● cocktail sticks.

1. Soak a sheet of newspaper in warm water. Squeeze the water out, and lay the paper flat on your baseboard.

▲2. Cover one side of the paper with wallpaper paste. Scrunch it up and knead it into a pulp. Repeat this process until you have enough pulp to model your castle's mound and courtyard. If you want to save time, mould your mound over an old plastic carton.

3. When your model is finished, leave it somewhere warm to dry.

TO MAKE A TOWER FOR THE MOUND

▲4. Fold a rectangle of corrugated card, as shown. Check that the outside ridges are vertical and that the four main panels are the same width.
Cut evenly spaced notches along the top of the tower, too.

TO MAKE THE ROOF

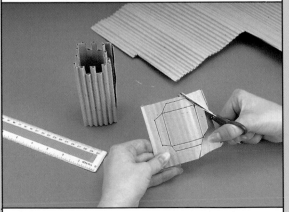

▲5. Draw a square with sides the same length as the width of one of the tower's panels. Add four tabs and cut this shape out.

▲ **6.** Fold the tabs down and smear them with glue. Now fold the tower around its roof. Make sure that the roof lies below the notches. Glue the rest of the tower together and paint it.

TO MAKE THE COURTYARD BUILDINGS

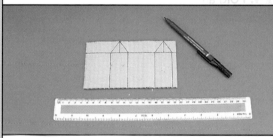

▲ **7.** Measure and mark a rectangle of corrugated card, as shown. The narrower panels must be the same width, as must the wider panels.

▲ **8.** Following your markings, cut away the top of the card. Cover the tab with glue and bend the building into shape.

TO MAKE THE ROOF

9. Cut out a small piece of card. Fold it in half and glue it into place.

10. When you have made as many buildings as you need, paint them. Stick dried grass, straw or twine onto their roofs.

11. When it has dried, paint your model and arrange the castle's buildings on it. Cut strips of corrugated card for fences and glue them into position.

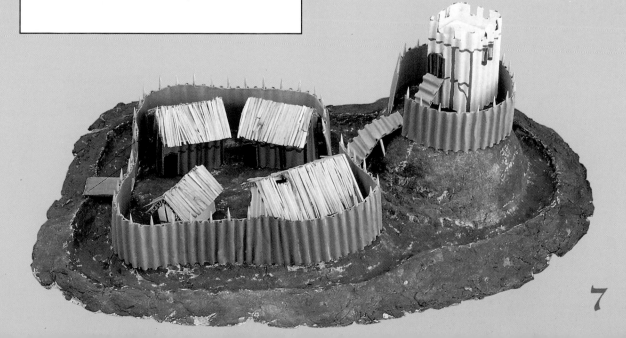

STONE STRONGHOLDS

No two castles built were ever exactly the same. Castle design varied according to where the castle was built, what it was built with, and who was in charge of its construction. Even so, like their wooden counterparts, many early stone castles were designed around one tall tower. These stone towers, later known as keeps, were the last retreat of the castle. They could be defended even if the thick curtain walls surrounding the castle had been breached.

The keep at Hedingham Castle in Essex is still standing, even though it was built in 1140. The cut-away picture below shows what it may have looked like when its lordly owner was home and entertaining important guests.

Because of the risk of fire, many castle kitchens were built in the courtyard instead of the keep.

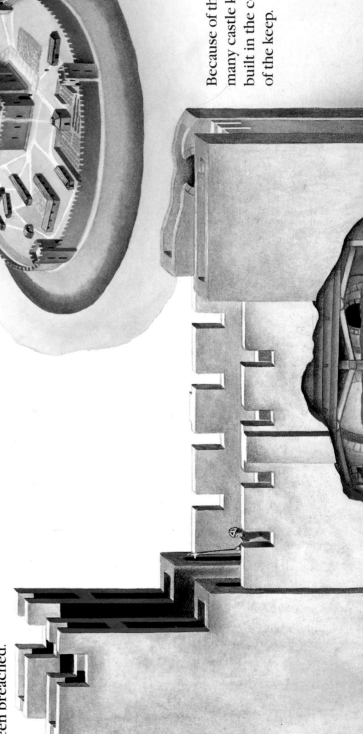

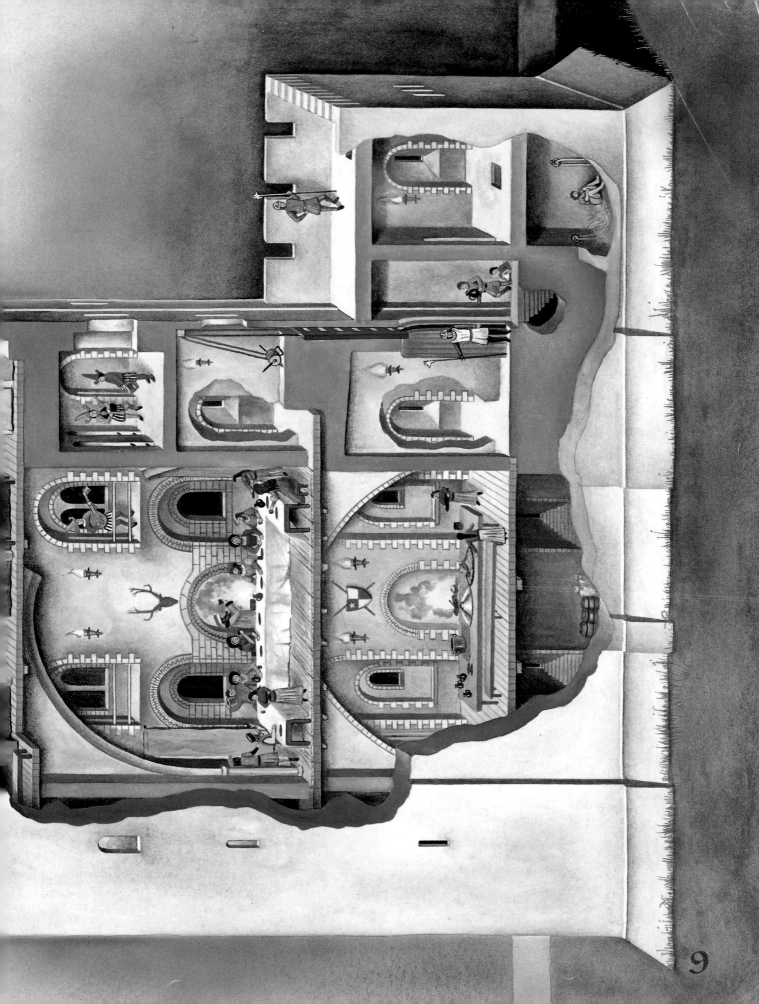

9

WELCOME TO HEDINGHAM

The main door was on the first floor to keep it beyond the reach of enemies with battering rams. Just to be on the safe side, it was also protected by a small tower and a wood and metal grating, called a portcullis. When unwanted visitors arrived, the portcullis was slid down from above, to block the doorway.

Troublemakers ended up in the dungeon! They were probably lowered to their doom through a trapdoor in the ceiling.

ON THE GROUND FLOOR

The ground floor was the ideal place for storing food and drink because it was cool and dark. With no heating, and walls 3.5 metres thick, the temperature was always low.

Unlike some keeps, Hedingham's had only one well. As there were no pipes and taps, the water had to be carried to wherever it was needed. When someone wanted a bath, water had to be hauled upstairs, heated over a fire and poured into a large wooden tub.

THE SPIRAL STAIRCASE

A keep's floors were connected by a spiral staircase. Hedingham's stairs wind upwards to the right. This may have helped a descending soldier if he had to fight his way down the stairs.

THE CONSTABLE'S ROOM AND THE LORD'S APARTMENT

The constable, who was in charge of the running of the castle, lived with his servants on the first floor. Here he greeted visitors and sorted out day-to-day castle business.

The most magnificent room of all was the lord's apartment, on the second floor. This was the room he used to carry out his public duties and to entertain formally. Rich tapestries hung on the walls to give the room colour and help stop draughts.

Far less magnificent, however, were the draughty toilets called garderobes. These were tiny rooms with chutes which ran through the walls and out into a pit at the bottom. The keep's floors were covered with rushes and sweet-smelling herbs to try and hide the terrible smell coming from the garderobes.

UP ON TOP

The lord, his family and their personal servants slept in the most private room of all, on the top floor. However, if the king came to stay, he would have been given this room, and the lord would have been relegated to the floor below.

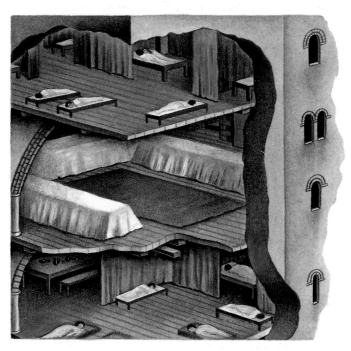

The higher floors had large windows because they were out of enemy and burglar reach. The lower floors had to have narrower windows, and arrow slits so that defending archers could fire out without enemy archers firing in.

MAKE YOUR OWN TAPESTRY

Tapestry in the Middle Ages was usually woven on a loom like this.

1. To make a simple loom, cut evenly spaced notches along the top and bottom edges of your piece of card.

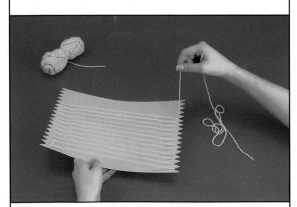

▲**2.** Wind some wool onto the card and knot the ends to the outside notches. These are the warp threads. They need to be pulled fairly taut so that the card bends slightly.

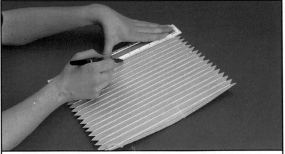

▲**3.** To keep the edges of your tapestry straight, draw lines inside the first and last warp threads. These lines will help you to see whether you are pulling your weaving too tight.

A thread that weaves in and out of the warp is called the weft.

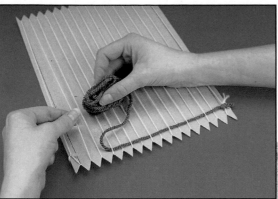

▲ 4. Tie your first weft to one of the outer warp threads. Weave it across the loom by going over and under alternate warp threads.

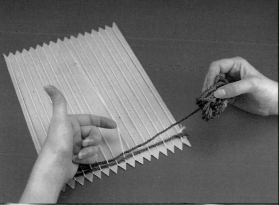

▲ 5. When you reach the final warp thread, weave the weft back again. This time it needs to go under and over alternately.

6. As you weave backwards and forwards, push the weft threads down firmly with your fingers. This will stop the warp showing through.

7. When you want to change colour or thread, knot the old and new weft threads together and push the knot to the back of your tapestry.

8. When you have finished, lift your weaving off its card loom. Slide a stick through the loops at the top and hang it up.

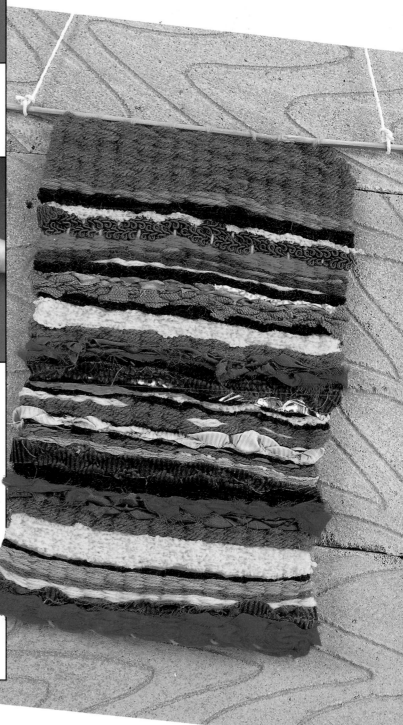

13

IN SEARCH OF THE PERFECT CASTLE

Castle design did not stop with the keep. As the Middle Ages progressed, many designers tried to keep attackers out of the castle courtyard by building stronger curtain walls. These walls had towers jutting out from them at fairly close intervals. This made it possible for archers to shelter in the towers and fire along the face of the wall.

Some of the larger wall towers were also turned into mini keeps. They provided extra accommodation and could be defended if the rest of the castle was captured.

A castle's weakest spot — its entrance — was also given a face lift. During the early 1200s, much mightier twin-towered gatehouses were built over the entrance. These gatehouses often had comfortable rooms upstairs where the constable in charge of the castle household might live.

The less welcoming entrance passage below was guarded by a drawbridge over the moat, wooden gates and at least one portcullis. "Murder holes" in the roof of the passage enabled defenders to drop missiles on the enemy, and to pour water on any fires they might have lit against the gates.

Sometimes the approach to a gatehouse was protected by a long narrow passage called a barbican. This made it difficult for large numbers of attackers to reach the gates or to smash through them with a battering ram.

A castle with such strong, well-protected outer walls and towers clearly had no need for a keep. Instead, the Great Hall, chapel, stores and kitchens were built inside the castle's courtyard, along with the rest of the domestic buildings. This arrangement gave everyone far more room than they would have had in a keep.

During the late 1200s, European castle designers started to build concentric castles. These had an open space at their centre and two sets of curtain walls. The inner wall overlooked the outer one. This enabled archers on the inner wall to fire at an approaching enemy over the heads of those defending the outer wall. If the enemy managed to cross the outer wall, he had no cover from the archers on the inner wall.

With every part defended by another part, concentric castles seemed almost impossible to capture.

▶ *Beaumaris is Britain's finest concentric castle.*

You will need: card ● scissors ● craft knife ● ruler ● pencil ● sticky tape ● plastic straw ● needle and thread ● plasticine ● thick paper ● paper clips ● paint ● pen ● some small cardboard boxes, for example, empty tea bag boxes ● gummed paper tape ● glue ● old toothbrush.

Ask a grown-up to help you with this, as the knife blade will be sharp!

Card is easier to fold if it has been scored first. To do this, gently run the tip of your craft knife along the line you want to fold. Use a ruler when scoring straight lines.

TO MAKE THE GATEHOUSE

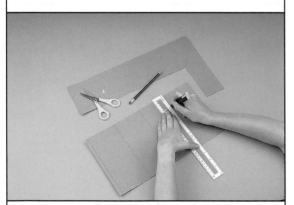

▲ I. Cut out a rectangle of card. Divide it into four panels with a tab at one end and then score all four lines.

2. To make battlements, cut evenly spaced notches along the top of the card.

▲ **3.** Cut a door into the bottom edge of the first and third panels.

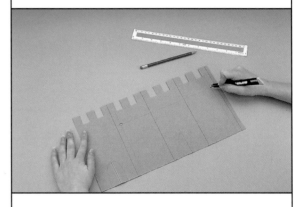

▲ **4.** Pierce a small hole into the left hand side of the second panel, and another into the right hand side of the fourth panel. The distance between each hole and its nearest panel must be the same. The distance between each hole and the base of the tower must also be the same.
The holes must be just big enough for a straw to fit through them.

5. Cover the tab with glue, fold the tower into shape and stick it together. Push a straw through both holes.

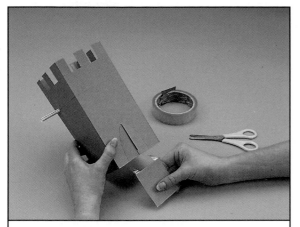

▲**6.** Cut out a small piece of card for the drawbridge. Use two tiny strips of sticky tape to attach it to the doorway furthest from the straw.

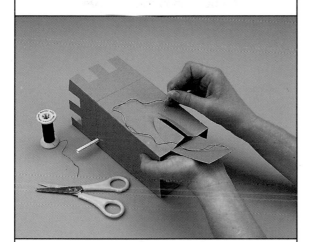

▲**7.** Thread a needle and knot the two loose ends of thread. Push the needle through one of the drawbridge's outer corners, and up through the front wall of the gatehouse.

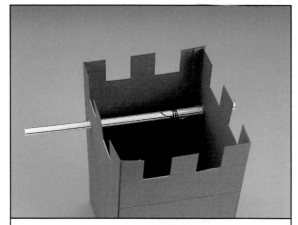

▲**8.** Lower the drawbridge and gently pull the thread straight. Now tape the rest of the thread to the straw. Make a second drawbridge rope in the same way.

9. Stick flattened strips of plasticine to the bottom of the drawbridge. It will now rise or lower when you turn both ends of the straw.

TO MAKE THE GATEHOUSE ROOF

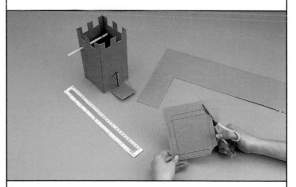

▲ **10.** Measure the width of one of your gatehouse's panels. Draw a square with sides this same length onto some card. Add four tabs and cut the shape out.

11. Score the lines you've drawn. Fold the tabs down, smear them with glue and stick the roof into place.

TO MAKE WALL TOWERS

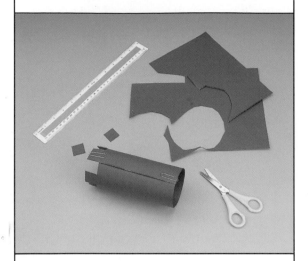

▲ 12. Cut battlements along the top of a rectangle of thick paper. Roll the paper into a tube and hold it together with paper clips.

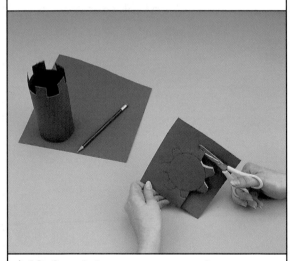

▲ 13. Stand the tower on another piece of thick paper and draw round it. Add tabs to your drawing and cut this shape out.

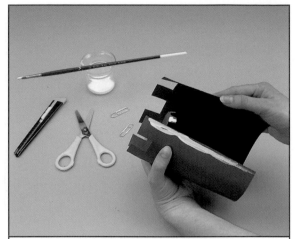

▲ 14. Score the circle and cover its tabs with glue. Fold the tower around its roof and glue the two free edges together.

TO MAKE WALLS

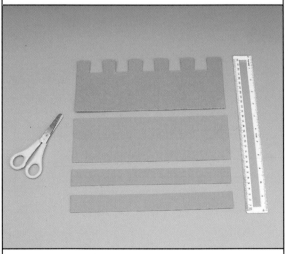

▲ 15. Cut battlements along the top of a long length of card.

Cut another piece of card, as long as the first but not quite as tall.

Cut two strips of card. They must be the same length as your first piece of card, but only a quarter of its height.

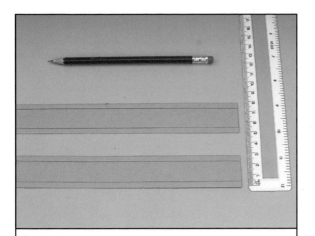

▲ **16.** Mark tabs along the longer edges of both of the thinner strips of card. All the tabs must be the same width.

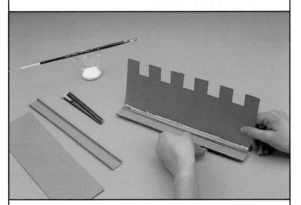

▲ **17.** Score all the lines you've drawn. Fold the tabs down, cover them with glue and stick all four lengths ▼ of card together, as shown.

18. When you have made all the walls and towers you need, join them together with gummed paper. Tape two tall towers on either side of the gatehouse.

▲ **19.** Now paint your model. If you want the walls to look speckled, cover everything around the castle, including the floor, with newspaper. Dip an old toothbrush in watery paint, and run your thumb towards you along the bristles. The paint will spatter onto the walls.

TO MAKE THE DOMESTIC BUILDINGS

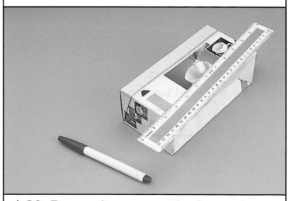

▲ **20.** Draw a line across the front of a small cardboard box. Then draw a diagonal line on each side of the box, as shown.
If the box has a lid, glue it shut.

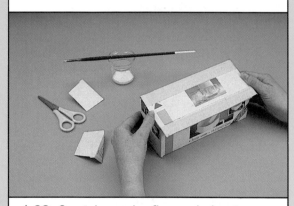

▲21. Cut along these lines and lift up the flap. Now cut away the triangular areas on each side of the flap.

▲22. Straighten the flap and glue it onto the lower section of the box. You may find that you need to trim this roof.

23. To make a hall with two sloping roofs, simply glue two box buildings back to back.

24. When you have made as many buildings as you need, paint them.

TO MAKE A MOAT

▶**25.** Stand your castle walls on a large sheet of blue card. Draw a squiggly line around the edge of the card. Draw a line round the inner walls of the castle's courtyard, too.

26. Remove the card from under the castle and cut along both lines. To finish, slide your moat into place and arrange the domestic buildings in the courtyard.

CASTLES UNDER ATTACK

TRICKS AND SURPRISES

The best way to capture a castle was to take it by surprise. In 1204, a French soldier terrified the inhabitants of Château Gaillard by climbing up a garderobe chute and letting his comrades in through a window. Imagine the shock of going to the toilet late one night, only to find someone climbing out of the seat!

GOING OVER THE TOP

Where a surprise attack failed, a direct assault might succeed. If the castle had a ditch, log tracks had to be built across it so that attackers with ladders could scale the walls.

Those who favoured a safer approach climbed tall wooden towers, called belfries. These were wheeled up to the castle wall so that the soldiers inside could storm their way over.

GROUND LEVEL ATTACK

Attackers often tried to smash through a castle's gate or corner walls with a heavy metal-tipped tree trunk, called a battering ram. They also tried to batter down the castle's walls using mangonels and trebuchets.

The mangonel was powered by twisted ropes. It could hurl great weights, but not very accurately!

The trebuchet, on the other hand, was deadly accurate. Developed during the 1100s, it had a sling at one end and a heavy counterweight at the other. When the counterweight fell, the missile in the sling went hurtling towards its target.

A large trebuchet could throw a dead horse. Bombarding a castle with rotting remains helped to spread disease amongst the defenders. Being splattered by foul horse flesh can't have done much for their morale either!

GOING UNDERGROUND

Castles without water-filled moats were vulnerable to tunnelling. Enemy miners would tunnel under a wall, set fire to the wooden poles used to support the tunnel's roof, and then wait for both the tunnel and the wall above it to collapse.

A WAITING GAME

Attackers sometimes tried to starve their enemy into surrender by mounting a siege. They camped outside the castle and stopped food from being delivered.

Sieges were not always successful, though. A well-stocked castle could survive for months, and many attackers dared not leave their own castles undefended for that long.

23

You will need: 2 blocks of balsa wood, 25mm square and 220mm long ● a large sheet of balsa (5mm thick) ● a stick of balsa wood about 220mm long ● unsharpened round pencil ● small screw hook ● matchbox ● string ● pebble ● sticky tape ● balsa cement ● craft knife ● small elastic band ● ruler ● paper.

Ask a grown-up to help you.

TO MAKE THE UPRIGHTS

1. Cut two pieces of balsa sheet, each measuring 110mm by 35mm. Carve a notch into one of the shorter sides of each piece. These notches must be wide enough and deep enough for the pencil to fit snugly into them.

▲**2.** Glue the uprights onto your two blocks of balsa wood, as shown. Make sure the notches line up with each other.

▲**3.** Cut a piece of balsa sheet 70mm by 15mm, and glue it across the front of the uprights. The position of this bar will affect your trebuchet's firing range.

▲**4.** Cut four pieces of balsa sheet, each 110mm by 20mm. Glue them, as shown, to complete the frame.

TO MAKE THE FIRING ARM

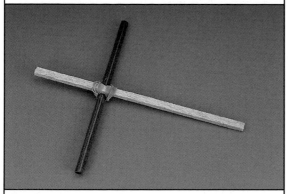

▲ **5.** Hold a pencil across your stick of balsa wood and fasten it with an elastic band. The pencil should be about a third of the way down the stick.

6. Tape a pebble to the short end of the arm. Glue half a matchbox tray to the other end.

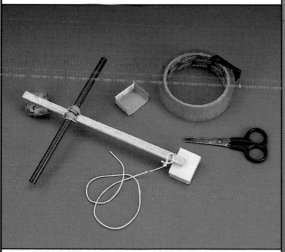

▲ **7.** Knot a length of string under the matchbox. Then tie a small loop in the string, near the knot.

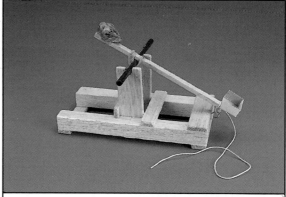

▲ **8.** Screw a small hook into the back of the frame. Rest the arm on the uprights and pull it down so that you can slip the loop of string over the hook.

9. To fire your trebuchet, put a crumpled ball of paper into the matchbox and flick the string off the hook.

CASTLES IN DECLINE

European castles went out of fashion because the society that had needed them began to change. In England and Wales this happened during the 1400s. As the monarchy grew stronger, private wars between great lords became less frequent. Pitched battles fought in the open countryside became more common. Since the two sides were often fighting to control the whole country, capturing a castle and its lands was not so important.

When cannons became popular weapons, soldiers were paid to man specially built gun forts. Fortress homes with their tall towers and arrow slits were no longer needed.

The times were changing in other ways, too. The nobility now longed for more comfortable homes, with bigger windows to let in more light. Some started to alter their castles accordingly. Others built grand manor houses instead. These new homes often had moats, battlements and gatehouses, but they were more for show than defence.

Castles that weren't adapted to a new role were abandoned. They were either pulled down and their building materials used for something else, or they were just left to crumble away.

▲ English gun fort, Deal, Kent.

Coity Castle in Wales fell into disuse at the end of the 1500s. ▼

Castle building survived longer in Scotland, Ireland and other parts of Europe than in England and Wales. In fact, when cannons became effective siege weapons, some European castles were adapted to withstand their fire. Walls were thickened, towers were lowered and their flat roofs were used as cannon platforms.

However, as gunfire became more effective and central governments became more stable, castles in the rest of Europe fell out of favour, too. Rather than turn their homes into gloomy gun forts, the rich wanted to live in princely palaces and magnificent mansions.

▲ *François I of France began building this expensive palace at Chambord in 1519.*

During the 1700s and 1800s, fairytale like castles became fashionable in parts of Europe. But, unlike the genuine castles of old, these were built for beauty, not defence.

▶ *Neuschwanstein Castle in Germany was built in 1869-92 by "Mad" King Ludwig II.*

CASTLES IN THE AIR

Castles have not only fascinated those interested in the past. They have spellbound story tellers, too. European myths and legends are full of tales about castles. The gods of Norse mythology lived in Asgard. This was a castle kingdom in the air, guarded by a massive rainbow bridge. The Welsh sea god, Manawyddan the Wise, lived in a castle made out of human bones.

Celtic mythology has many stories about castles buried beneath the sea. One myth recalls the watery fate of the castle of Y's, in Cornwall. The people of Y's grew so unbelievably wicked that one day the sea rose up and swallowed their castle and town. They will only be saved when a young man on the mainland hears the sad sound of the castle's chapel bell.

As castles disappeared from the real world, story tellers started inventing more and more weird and wonderful ones to take their place. Some are dark and disturbing, like the devilish castle created by the Italian writer, Dante. In his castle, everything is horribly reversed. The moat is a river of death. The burning hot walls are designed to keep people in, not out. The curtain walls spiral inwards and downwards to a pit filled with horrors.

Some of the most popular stories of all have real castles at their centre. William Shakespeare's play *Macbeth* is set in Glamis Castle, in Scotland. His play *Hamlet* takes place at the royal castle of Elsinore, in Denmark.

Glamis Castle has a bloody history, both in fact and fiction. ▼

▲ *Kronborg Castle in Denmark was made famous by the play Hamlet.*

There is a German legend about a young man called Dietrich who rescues a princess from a dwarf king's castle, only to find that the ungrateful girl prefers her captor to him. The story goes that this castle can be found in the Tyrolean mountains. However, since only the pure and good can see it, it's unlikely that anyone has ever had a quick look inside!

29

GLOSSARY

Armourer — the man who looked after the castle's weapons and armour.

Barbican — some barbicans were like long walkways leading to the gatehouse. Others were like small gatehouses, built to protect the bridge leading to the main gatehouse.

Battering ram — a metal-tipped tree trunk or wooden pole, which was often suspended from the roof of a wooden shed on wheels. By swinging the ram to and fro against the castle's gate or corners, a team of men could smash their way through to the other side.

Battlements — a line of notches along the top of a tower or wall. Defending archers fired between the gaps, called crenels, and hid behind the higher bits of stonework, called merlons.

Belfries — tall wooden siege towers on wheels. They were often topped by a drawbridge and covered with animal hides for fireproofing.

Celts — an ancient race of people who came from western Britain, Wales, Ireland, Scotland and Brittany.

Château Gaillard — the favourite castle of King Richard I of England. It was built in the 1190s, on a cliff overlooking the River Seine, in France.

Curtain wall — general name given to the wall and towers surrounding a castle.

Legends — traditional stories that are part fact and part fiction. Myths and legends are handed down from one generation to the next.

Mangonel — a catapult used for throwing stones great distances when attacking a castle.

Myth — an ancient traditional story. Myths are often about gods and heroes. Many have a religious meaning, or try to explain some scientific fact.

Mythology — the study of myths; a collection of the myths and legends of a particular culture.

Norse mythology — the myths and legends of the Vikings, who came from Scandinavia.

Pitched battle — one that has been arranged and is fought on a chosen site.

Reed — a tall, stiff marsh or water grass.

Rushes — grass-like plants that grow near marshes.

Trebuchet — a large wooden catapult used when attacking a castle.

RESOURCES

PLACES TO VISIT

There are many castles in Britain open to the public. To find those nearest to you, contact your local tourist board or write to one of the following:

The National Trust (Headquarters)
36 Queen Anne's Gate
London SW1H 9AS

The National Trust for Scotland
5 Charlotte Square
Edinburgh

Cadw: Welsh Historic Monuments
Brunel House
Fitzalan Road
Cardiff CF2 1UY

Full details of all English Heritage castles, including opening times, are given in the Guide To English Heritage Properties. For your copy, write to:
English Heritage,
PO Box 43, Ruislip,
Middlesex HA4 0XW.
(enclose £1.95, plus 35p for postage).

Mountfitchet Castle in Stansted, Essex is a reconstructed 11th century timber castle. For further details, telephone 0279 813237.

For further information about Hedingham Castle, contact:
Castle Hedingham
Halstead
Essex CO9 3DJ
Tel: Hedingham (0787) 60261

BOOKS TO READ

Non Fiction
Castles by Jenny Vaughan, Franklin Watts 1984.

Inside story, A Medieval Castle by Fiona Macdonald and Mark Bergin, Simon and Schuster 1990.

See *Inside a Castle* by R. J. Unstead, Kingfisher Books 1986.

Medieval Castles by Brian Adams, Gloucester Press 1989.

Fiction
The Age of Chivalry, myths and legends, Cherrytree Books. (Myths and legends set in the age of castles).

Island of the Mighty: Stories of Old Britain by Hayden Middleton and Anthea Toorchen, Oxford University Press. (Re-telling of Welsh legends).

GAMES TO PLAY

You can get the following software from Rickett Educational Media, Ilton, Somerset TA19 9BR:

Fletcher's Castle — a Norman knight tries to build a timber castle in ten days.

Castle Under Attack — a strategy game for 9-14 year olds.

INDEX

Additional photographs: Bridgeman Art Library/Private Collection 4(b); Danish Tourist Board 29(t); Michael Holford 26(t), 27(t); Hutchison Library 4(t); Science Museum 12(t); Wales Tourist Board 14, 26(b); Zefa 27(b), 29(b).